PULLEYS
AND GEARS

ANGELA ROYSTON

www.heinemann.co.uk.
Visit our website to find out more information about Heinemann Library books

To order:
 Phone ++44 (0)1865 888066
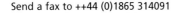 Send a fax to ++44 (0)1865 314091
 Visit the Heinemann Bookshop at www.heinemann.co.uk to browse our catalogue and order online.

First published in Great Britain by Heinemann Library,
Halley Court, Jordan Hill, Oxford OX2 8EJ,
a division of Reed Educational and Professional Publishing Ltd.
Heinemann is a registered trademark of Reed Educational & Professional Publishing Limited.

OXFORD MELBOURNE AUCKLAND
JOHANNESBURG BLANTYRE GABORONE
IBADAN PORTSMOUTH NH (USA) CHICAGO

© Reed Educational and Professional Publishing Ltd 2000

Designed by Visual Image
Illustrations by Barry Atkinson
Originated by Dot Gradations
Printed in Hong Kong/China

04 03 02 01 00
10 9 8 7 6 5 4 3 2 1

ISBN 0431 01743 3

British Library Cataloguing in Publication Data

Royston, Angela
  Pulleys and gears. - (How it works)
  1.Pulleys - Juvenile literature 2.Gearing - Juvenile literature
  I.Title
  621.8'3

Acknowledgements

The Publishers would like to thank the following for permission to reproduce photographs: National Motor Museum p14; Corbis: p26; Eye Ubiquitous: Bruce Adams p7; Heinemann: Trevor Clifford pp13, 16, 17, 20, 21, 23, 28, 29; Photodisk: p18; Pictor Uniphoto: p4, p10, 24; Tony Stone Images: Lori Adamski Peek p5, Keith Wood p9, Tom Montgomery p22

Cover photograph reproduced with permission of Science Photo Library.

The Publishers would like to thank Anthony Mirams for his help and advice with the text and Jo Brooker for making the models on p28-9.

Every effort has been made to contact copyright holders of any material reproduced in this book. Any omissions will be rectified in subsequent printings if notice is given to the Publisher.

Any words appearing in the text in bold, **like this**, are explained in the Glossary.

CONTENTS

What are pulleys and gears?

The pulleys on the deck of this fishing boat help the fishermen pull in their catch.

Pulleys and **gears** use wheels to make it easier to do some things, such as lift heavy loads. Wheels, pulleys and gears are simple machines. This book looks at how they work and how they are used.

A wheel allows you to use a small **force** to produce a big result. For example, wheels are often used to make it easier to carry things. Pulleys and gears are special kinds of wheels. A pulley is a wheel with a groove round the outside for a rope or cable to fit into. Gears use one wheel to turn another.

A mountain bike has many toothed gear wheels around the hub of the back wheel. The gears help the cyclist to pedal up and down steep hills.

Gears

Gear wheels have teeth around their **rims** which fit into each other. So when one wheel turns, it turns any other wheel that is linked to it. The gears on a mountain bike allow the bike to go faster or slower while the cyclist pedals at the same speed.

Think about it!

Can you guess which of these don't use a pulley or gear wheels? An egg whisk, a tin opener, a television, a sewing machine, a kettle, a clock.

A simple pulley

The simplest kind of pulley is a rope or cord pulled over the branch of a tree, or a smooth beam.

No one knows who invented the **pulley**, but the first pulleys were probably simply a rope thrown over a smooth branch. Someone must have discovered that a **load** tied to one end was then easier to lift.

The rope over the tree works because it allows you to pull down in order to lift something up. Pulling down is easier than pulling up because you can use your weight to help you. A wheel at the top works better than the branch because there is less **friction** and so the rope slides more easily.

Make it work!

Use a simple pulley to lift a weight. Tie a piece of strong string or cord around a large, thick book or house brick. Lift the book with the string using one hand. Now put the string over the back of a chair and pull the string down with one hand to lift the book. Which way is easier?

Flag pole

A small, **grooved** wheel hangs from the top of the flag pole. The flag is tied to a long loop of thin rope, which fits into the groove of the wheel. As you pull one side of the loop down, the other side goes up, taking the flag with it.

When you raise a flag on a flag pole, you pull down one rope and up goes the flag.

Block and tackle

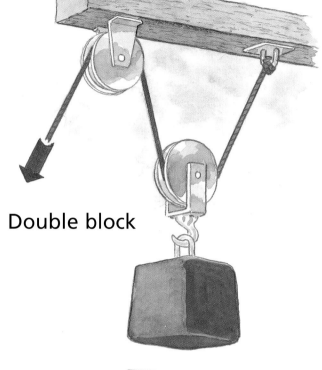

Double block

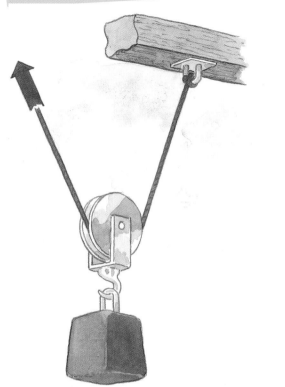

Single block

The wheel of a **pulley** does not have to be fixed to the highest point of the machine. The **load** itself can be hung from a hook that is joined to the pulley. This is called a **block**. A single block has one wheel, and a double block has two wheels.

Using two pulley wheels together allows you to lift heavier loads with the same amount of effort.

A double block uses the same amount of pull to lift a load that is twice as heavy. So it takes the same amount of pull to lift 10 kilograms with a single block as it does to lift 20 kilograms with a double block.

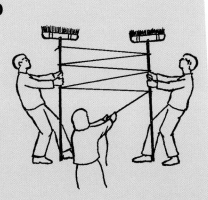

This system of
pulleys is called a
block and tackle. It
uses a very long
rope threaded over
several pulleys to lift
a heavy load.

pulley

pulleys

Many blocks

The more blocks a machine uses, the heavier
the loads it can lift. A machine with ten
pulleys will lift ten times the load with the
same amount of pull. Using this machine, one
person can lift the heavy pipe.

A tower crane

The hook on a tower crane is lowered to pick up a heavy load. The crane is operated by the cab driver. He moves the hook to lift the load from one place to another.

A tower crane can lift a very heavy **load**. It is operated by a driver in a cab, right at the top of the crane. The load is hung from a hook which hangs from a long steel cable. One end of the cable passes over a **pulley** and is attached to the end of the crane's long **jib**. The other end of the cable passes over two more pulleys and then is wound around a **winch**. The winch is turned by a powerful motor. It winds the cable up and down.

The trolley

The pulleys above the load are attached to a **trolley**, which helps to take the load to where it has to go. The trolley rolls on wheels along the jib and is moved by two separate steel cables and pulleys. The cables are wound in and released by a trolley winch.

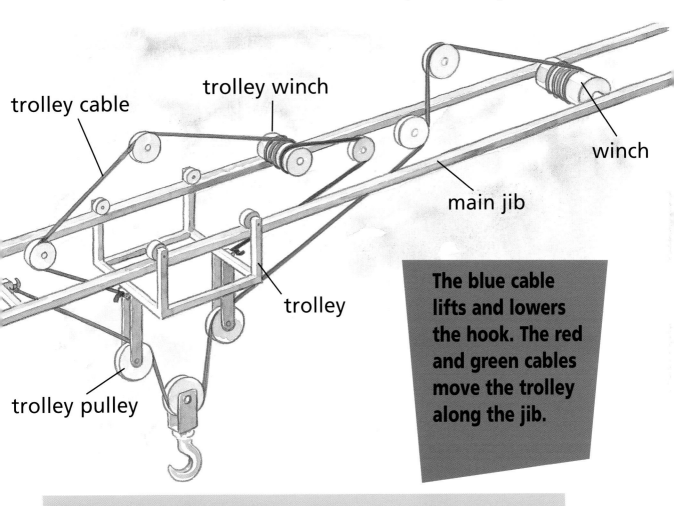

trolley winch

trolley cable

winch

main jib

trolley

The blue cable lifts and lowers the hook. The red and green cables move the trolley along the jib.

trolley pulley

Did you know?

A crane has to be taller than the skyscraper being built. Some tower cranes are erected alongside the building, but others are situated in the middle of the skyscraper. As the building gets higher, the crane is built higher too.

Drive belts

The chain on a bicycle takes the power of the moving pedals to the hub of the back wheel.

A **drive belt** is a belt which is looped around at least two **pulleys**. When one pulley is turned, the other is turned too. In many machines, one pulley is attached to an **axle** and is turned by a motor. The belt then turns the second pulley and moves another part of the machine.

The chain on a bicycle is a kind of drive belt. The pedals turn a large wheel which is joined by the chain to the small **hub** of the back wheel. As the pedals turn round slowly, the chain pulls the back wheel around fast. The back wheel moves the bicycle forwards.

Different arrangements

When a drive belt links two wheels of the same size, both wheels turn at the same speed. But if one wheel is smaller than the other, the small wheel turns much faster than the large wheel. If the smaller pulley is half the size of the other, it will turn twice as fast.

same size – same speed

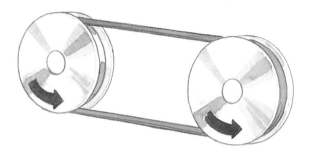

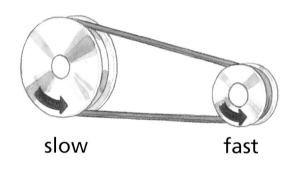

slow   fast

crossed belt

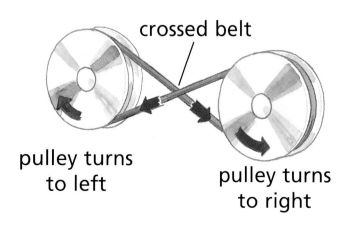

pulley turns to left

pulley turns to right

Drive belts in action

A fan belt is used to keep a car engine cool.

fan belt

Drive belts are used in cars, sewing machines, and many other machines. In the early steam tractor the wheel on the top of the vehicle was connected to the back wheel of the tractor. As the wheels turned, the tractor moved forward.

Drive belts can be powered by all kinds of engines, such as electric motors and petrol engines. Some cars have a fan belt, which uses the movement of the engine to turn a fan. The fan sucks in cool air to keep the radiator cool.

Make it work!

Design a machine which uses a drive belt to turn a children's roundabout. Will you make one wheel bigger than the other, and if so, which one?

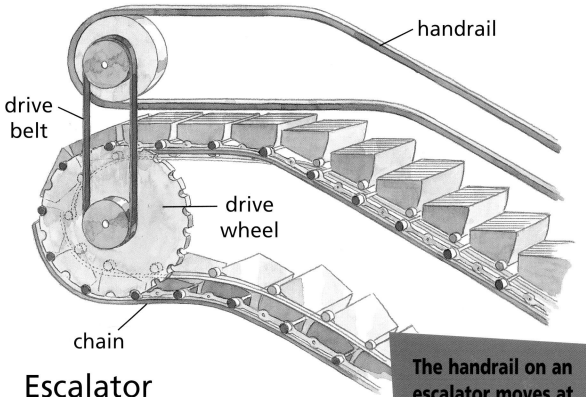

handrail

drive belt

drive wheel

chain

Escalator

The metal stairs of an escalator are connected to a chain that is moved around by a drive wheel. At the top of the escalator, the stairs flatten out and bend around the drive wheel. They then travel down behind the escalator to the bottom to start again. To make the escalator move down rather than up, the drive wheel is turned in the opposite direction.

The handrail on an escalator moves at the same pace as the stairs. What would happen if the upper wheel in the drive belt was smaller than the lower wheel?

15

Gears

Gear wheels that touch move in opposite directions. If the biggest wheel moves round clockwise, which way will the smallest wheel turn?

A round **gear** wheel has notched teeth around the **rim**. It is called a **spur gear**. A gear kit has several spur wheels, some bigger than others. Although the wheels are different sizes, the teeth are the same size so that they fit together. As the big wheel turns, its teeth push the teeth of the smaller wheel around.

Think about it!

Which wheels will turn at the same speed as the yellow wheels? Which wheels will turn more than twice as fast as the red wheels? (Count the teeth to find out.)

Gear train

A gear train is when one spur gear is used to turn several other spur gears. If the wheels in the train are the same size, they turn at the same speed. If one wheel is smaller than the other, it will turn faster. You have to compare the number of teeth to see how much faster one wheel will turn than the other. If the larger wheel has double the number of teeth, the small wheel will turn twice as fast.

How fast a gear wheel turns depends on the number of teeth it has. Small gear wheels move faster than large gear wheels.

17

Clocks and watches

Most clocks and watches today are worked by **quartz crystals**, but you can still find some mechanical clocks and watches. The minute hand makes one complete turn every hour, while the hour hand takes 12 hours to make one complete turn. They are worked by a spring, which you wind up, and by **spur gears**.

Did you know?

The first mechanical clocks had no hands. They rang a bell to show the hours and so were built in tall clock towers. People listened out for the bells because they had no other way of knowing the time.

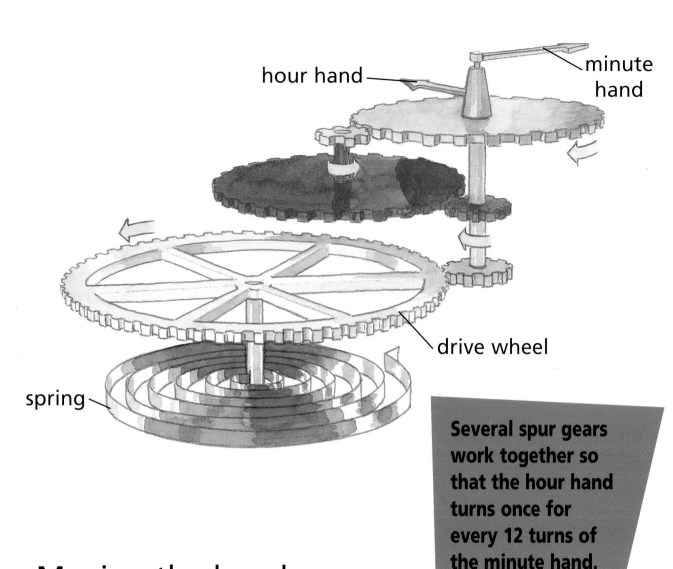

hour hand

minute hand

drive wheel

spring

Several spur gears work together so that the hour hand turns once for every 12 turns of the minute hand.

Moving the hands

The spring slowly unwinds to make the driving wheel turn. The minute hand is joined to the small green spur gear and it makes one complete turn every hour.

The small red wheel on the minute hand turns the large red wheel. The large red wheel makes one complete turn every three hours. The small blue wheel also turns once every three hours. It turns the large blue wheel which is joined to the hour hand. It makes a complete turn every 12 hours.

Bevel gears

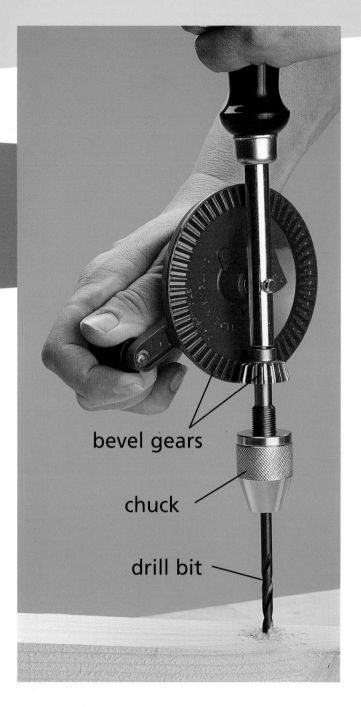

When you turn the handle of the hand drill, the **drill bit** spins around very fast. The **chuck** holds the bit tightly so that it will not fly off. The bit spins fast because the **gear** wheel on the handle is larger than the gear wheels on the chuck.

bevel gears

chuck

drill bit

The gears on the chuck have sloping teeth and are called **bevel gears**. They allow you to turn the handle in one direction to make the drill bit spin in a different direction.

20

Think about it!

See how a bevel gear changes the direction of spin. Use your finger to trace in the air the direction the handle of the drill bit turns (like a bicycle wheel in front of you). Now use your finger to trace the way the drill bit turns.

When you turn the handle of the whisk, the blades go round in opposite directions. Why do the blades not hit each other?

Egg whisk

A whisk is used to beat eggs until they are frothy, or to thicken cream. The whisk uses bevel gears. The blades are attached to a small gear wheel on each side of a large wheel. Watch carefully as you turn the handle of the whisk to see how the small bevel gears spin in opposite directions. The blades are carefully positioned so that they fit into the spaces between each other. Each time the handle turns around once, the small gears spin around four times.

Changing direction

The angler flicks the long rod and the line arches out over the water. A skilful angler can get the hooks to land just where he wants them. When a fish bites, he turns a handle on the rod to reel the line in. The **bevel gears** inside the handle allow him to cast and reel in smoothly. The handle turns a large gear wheel which turns a small bevel gear. The small **gear** wheel winds in the fishing line.

The angler has to wind in the fish smoothly and slowly so that the fish does not fall off the line. Bevel gears inside the handle work the winder.

Worm gear

A gear which looks like a screw is called a **worm gear**. The round wheel is a **spur gear**. The worm gear turns very fast to make the spur wheel turn very slowly. For example, the speedometer in a car measures how fast the wheels are turning and how far the car has gone. Worm gears change the fast spin of the wheels into a much slower movement, so that the milometer turns just one notch every tenth of a mile.

A worm gear looks like a screw and fits into a spur gear. Although the worm gear turns very fast, the spur gear turns very slowly.

Think about it!

A worm gear gives slow, controlled movement. Which of these would you use a worm gear for – flying a kite, lifting a wheelchair on and off a bus, pulling up an anchor?

Bicycles

Many bikes have **gears** to make it easier to cycle up hills. Pedalling turns the chain on a simple bicycle, but the back wheel has several different sized toothed wheels around the **hub**. These special gear wheels are called **sprockets**. When you select a gear using the lever on the handlebars, the chain connects with one of the sprockets.

Mountain bikes have several gears which allow the rider either to cycle very slowly or very fast. Some mountain bikes have 28 gears.

24

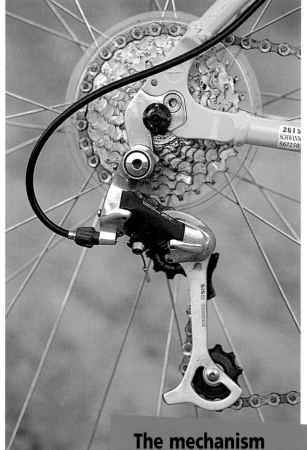

Did you know?

Track racing bikes have only one gear. This is because racing is done on an evenly sloped track. The cyclists try to outwit each other, but they do not need lots of gears – they either cycle at full speed or free wheel.

The mechanism which shifts the chain from one gear wheel to another is called a derailleur. It is controlled by a lever on the handlebar or frame.

Low and high gears

If you choose a low gear, the chain connects with a large sprocket. This means that the back wheel turns around more slowly as you pedal. In other words it takes less effort to turn the back wheel. Low gears are useful when you start moving and when you are cycling uphill.

When you change to a higher gear, the chain connects with a smaller sprocket. This means that the back wheel turns faster, while the pedals turn at the same speed. High gears are useful for going fast along flat ground.

Gears in action

Gears may be tiny, like the ones in a delicate watch, or huge, like the ones shown here in the mill. They may be made of wood, metal or plastic. They may be driven by the winding of a handle, by a motor or by the wind or water.

Wind and watermills used the power of wind and water to turn the gear wheels. They were invented over a thousand years ago and were the first machines that did not need people or animals to make them turn.

In a windmill the wind blows the sails around. Gears use the turning of the sails to turn the big wheel in the photo. As it turns around slowly, a smaller wheel turns fast and turns the grindstone. Grains of wheat are fed between the two grindstones to be ground into flour.

Make it work!

Draw a design for a machine (but not a vehicle) that uses several gears to make it work at different speeds. You could perhaps design an exercise machine for a hamster or for a human. You do not have to draw the gears in detail, just the machine.

gear lever

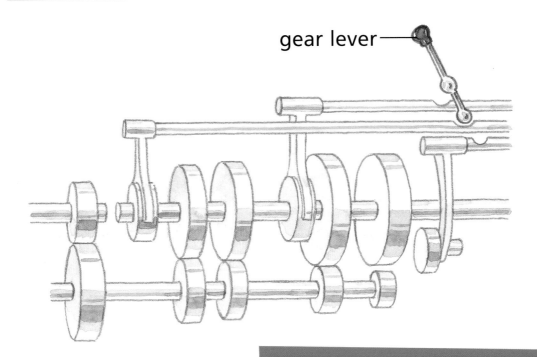

The driver of a car changes gear as the car goes faster. The engine still works at the same speed, but the higher gear turns the wheels faster.

Gears in use

The gear box of a car allows the engine to turn at more or less the same speed, while the wheels start off turning slowly and end up turning very fast. As the driver moves the gear lever in the car, the lever moves from one rod to another. Each rod sets in motion a different selection of gear wheels.

Make a toy windmill

This windmill uses two **pulleys** and a **drive belt** to turn the sails.

You will need:

thin card
tracing paper
stapler
an empty shoe box
ballpoint pen
2 pieces of wooden dowel, about 8 mm in diameter
one or two large wide rubber bands
masking tape
scissors, ruler, pencil

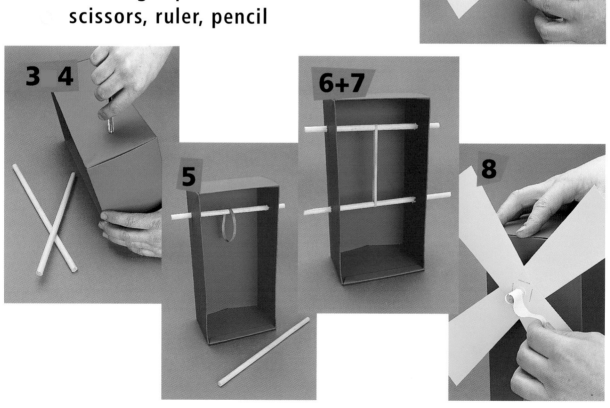

1 Make four sails by tracing the shape of the sail onto the card. Cut out the shapes and the hole at one end.

2 Staple the four sails together so that they make a cross and the holes line up.

3 Cut one piece of dowel so that it is 4 cm longer than the width of the box. Cut the other piece so that it is 8 cm longer than the width of the box.

4 Use the pen to make a hole through one side of the box, 5 cm from one end as shown. Make a similar hole in the other side, 5 cm from the same end. If necessary, use the blade of the scissors to widen the holes so that the dowel slips through easily.

5 Put the shorter piece of dowel through one hole and place the rubber band around it before pushing the dowel through the hole in the other side of the box. Wind masking tape around the ends to stop them slipping back through the holes (but do not prevent the dowel from turning).

6 Pull the rubber band taut and measure where it comes to on the side of the box. Make a hole on each side, as you did in Step 4. Thread the longer piece of dowel through the holes, taking in the rubber band in the middle.

7 Turn the lower dowel to check whether the rubber band turns with it and turns the top dowel too. You may find it works better if you put two rubber bands between the dowels rather than one.

8 Slide the sails over the upper dowel and use masking tape to fix them to the dowel.

9 When you turn the lower dowel the sails should go round.

Glossary

axle a rod or bar joined to the hub of a wheel

beam a large, heavy rod or bar

bevel gear gear with sloping teeth that changes the angle of turn

block a hook attached to a pulley that can move

block and tackle a set of fixed and moving pulleys that work together

chuck the part of a drill that holds the drill bit

drill bit the spinning screw on the end of a drill

drive belt a loop that links one pulley to another

force a push, pull or twist that makes something move

friction rubbing between two surfaces which slows down speed

gear a toothed wheel which fits into another toothed wheel to change the speed or direction of the circular movement

groove a narrow channel cut by a machine

hub the centre of a wheel

jib the long arm of a crane which carries the hook

load the weight or force that a lever moves or balances

pulley a simple machine which uses a wheel and rope to make lifting easier

quartz crystals tiny pieces of stone which are used to regulate clocks and watches

rim the outer edge

sprocket toothed wheel on the pedals and bike wheel of a bike

spur gear round, flat gear with teeth around the edge

trolley a car hung from a pulley which moves on an overhead wire

winch a machine for winding and unwinding a rope or cable

worm gear a gear with a spiral thread like a screw

Answers to questions

p5 A television and a kettle do not use either pulleys or gears. Tin openers in which you turn a handle to move the opener around the tin use a gear, but some kinds of tin opener just have a sharp blade.

p12 When you turn one bottle, the cord should turn the other bottle in the same direction. When the cord is crossed the other bottle turns in the opposite direction from the first.

p14 If the **pulley** attached to the roundabout is bigger than the pulley attached to the engine or the handle, the roundabout will turn slowly while the engine or handle turns fast.

p15 Escalator picture: if the upper wheel was smaller, the hand rail would move faster than the stairs.

p16 Gear train picture: the smallest wheel would move in the opposite direction – anti-clockwise.

p17 The green and the blue wheels turn at the same speed as the yellow wheels. The purple wheels have six teeth and so will turn more than twice as fast as the red wheels which have 14 teeth.

p21 The blades are carefully positioned so that they fit into the spaces between each other.

p23 A **worm gear** would be useful for lifting a wheelchair onto a bus.

Index

Titles in the *How it Works* series include:

Hardback   0 431 01742 5

Hardback   0 431 01744 1

Hardback   0 431 01743 3

Hardback   0 431 01745 X

Hardback   0 431 01747 6

Hardback   0 431 01746 8

Find out about the other titles in this series on our website www.heinemann.co.uk/library